Grizzly Bears

Therese Shea

Gareth Stevens
Publishing

Please visit our Web site, www.garethstevens.com. For a free color catalog of all our high-quality books, call toll free 1-800-542-2595 or fax 1-877-542-2596.

Library of Congress Cataloging-in-Publication Data

Shea, Therese.
Grizzly bears / Therese Shea.
    p. cm. – (Animals that live in the tundra)
Includes index.
 ISBN 978-1-4339-3900-6 (pbk.)
 ISBN 978-1-4339-3901-3 (6-pack)
 ISBN 978-1-4339-3899-3 (library binding)
1. Grizzly bear—Juvenile literature. I. Title.
QL737.C27S476 2011
599.784–dc22

                                        2010012655

First Edition

Published in 2011 by
Gareth Stevens Publishing
111 East 14th Street, Suite 349
New York, NY 10003

Copyright © 2011 Gareth Stevens Publishing

Designer: Michael J. Flynn
Editor: Therese Shea

Photo credits: Cover, pp. 1, 5, 7, 9, 11, 13, 15, 17, 19, 21, back cover Shutterstock.com.

Printed in the United States of America

CPSIA compliance information: Batch #CS10GS: For further information contact Gareth Stevens, New York, New York at 1-800-542-2595.

Table of Contents

Boldface words appear in the glossary.

Big Brown Bears

Grizzly bears are huge brown bears. They live in many parts of North America, including the cold **tundra** of Canada and Alaska.

Grizzlies have brown fur with light-colored tips. A grizzly has a hump on its back. The hump is **muscle** that helps the grizzly run and dig.

hump

Big Eaters

A grizzly bear cannot see well. However, it can smell food that is miles away. Grizzlies eat nuts, fruit, leaves, berries, grasses, and roots.

Grizzly bears also eat small animals, such as **rodents**, fish, and bugs. They sometimes eat young moose. Grizzlies eat dead animals, too.

Grizzlies have claws. Each claw is as long as a person's finger! They use their claws to dig for food. They also dig holes to store food.

claw

Grizzlies like to be alone. To keep others away, they mark their land. They bite and claw trees and rub against them. Grizzlies may eat together in places with a lot of food.

Grizzlies eat a lot in summer.
They store fat in their bodies.
They dig dens in the fall.
Then they **hibernate** through
the long, cold winter.

Family Talk

Mother grizzlies have cubs
in January or February.
Many cubs are twins. Mother
grizzlies talk to their cubs.
They growl, moan, and grunt.

cubs

Grizzly bears can be very **dangerous**. Mother grizzlies may be the most dangerous of all. They will **attack** people to keep their cubs safe.

Fast Facts

Height	up to 3.5 feet (1.1 meters) at shoulders
Length	up to 8 feet (2.4 meters)
Weight	up to 800 pounds (365 kilograms)
Diet	rodents, bugs, fish, and young moose; leaves, berries, fruit, nuts, grasses, and roots
Average life span	up to 25 years

Glossary

attack: to try to harm

dangerous: likely to cause harm

hibernate: to sleep most of the winter while living off body fat

muscle: a part of the body that helps it move

rodent: a small animal with large teeth, such as a mouse, rat, or squirrel

tundra: flat, treeless plain with ground that is always frozen

For More Information

Books

Miles, Elizabeth. *Watching Grizzly Bears in North America.* Chicago, IL: Heinemann Library, 2006.

Moody-Luther, Jacqueline. *Grizzly Bear Cub.* Norwalk, CT: Soundprints, 2006.

Web Sites

Grizzly Bear
www.nwf.org/Wildlife/Wildlife-Library/Mammals/ Grizzly-Bear.aspx
Read about grizzlies, including more about hibernation and grizzly cubs.

Grizzly Bear
animals.nationalgeographic.com/animals/mammals/ grizzly-bear
See a map and read about grizzly bear history.

Index

About the Author

Therese Shea is an editor and author of many children's nonfiction books. A graduate of Providence College, she has an M.A. in English Education from the University at Buffalo. She lives and works in Buffalo, New York.